Henry Berkowitz

Kiddush; or, Sabbath Sentiment in the Home

Henry Berkowitz

Kiddush; or, Sabbath Sentiment in the Home

ISBN/EAN: 9783743350182

Manufactured in Europe, USA, Canada, Australia, Japa

Cover: Foto ©ninafisch / pixelio.de

Manufactured and distributed by brebook publishing software
(www.brebook.com)

Henry Berkowitz

Kiddush; or, Sabbath Sentiment in the Home

KIDDUSH

OR

Sabbath Sentiment

IN THE HOME.

By HENRY BERKOWITZ, D. D.

Rabbi Cong. RODEPH SHALOM, Philadelphia, Pa

WITH SPECIAL ILLUSTRATIONS BY
KATHERINE M. COHEN.

"The Sabbath is the hub of the Jew's universe ; to protract
it is a virtue; to love it a liberal education."
—I. ZANGWILL.

PHILADELPHIA, PENN.,
1898.

Second Thousand.

TO THE WOMEN OF ISRAEL,

In the firm assurance that it lies with
them to awaken the religious
life and enkindle the Jewish
spirit by fostering the
Sabbath Sentiment
within their
hearts and
homes.

A SUGGESTION.

That was a beautiful custom which our sires observed, but which has fallen sadly into disuse in these modern times. Every Friday evening the Jew would return to his home from the Synagogue, perhaps weary after the week's toil, but with his heart all aglow with love for his dear ones who were eagerly awaiting his coming. From afar he could see the Sabbath light radiating from his home, beckoning him cheerily and lovingly. Upon his arrival at home his wife and children would greet him with beaming faces, and receive his blessing in reverential attitude. Then, after all were seated about the festal board, the husband proceeded to usher in the Sabbath by reading to his wife that gem of Hebrew literature, "Esheth Hayil," The Virtuous Woman. (Proverbs, XXXI, 10-31.)

We can readily understand that the reading of this poem, week after week, on the Sabbath eve, whenever the exercise was not a barren and meaningless formality, would exert an ennobling influence, not alone upon the wife and mother, but upon the husband and children as well. Before the minds of the women in the Jewish home this poem set up a lofty ideal of wife and motherhood, above all, of womanhood. To her who was conscious of striving after this noble pattern, the reading of it by the husband must have come as a loving recognition of her merits and an encouragement to persist in her endeavor. To the woman, however, who fell short of these attainments, it must have come each week as a new impetus for better effort.

Recognizing these far-reaching effects upon the Jewish home and all its inmates and having drawn so much comfort and inspiration out of these observances in our own home, I was eager to see them spread into all Jewish households that are deprived of this beautiful ceremony. I therefore urged my husband to arrange a simple little home service for the Sabbath eve, which would preserve the spirit of the old "Kiddush" and yet adapt the form to our modern needs.

In compliance with this wish this little book is now sent forth. May it receive a hearty welcome in every Jewish household and help to restore and sustain one of the most simple and effective usages for "carrying on the chain of piety that links the generations to each other."

FLORA BERKOWITZ.

INTRODUCTORY.

What a work of genius is that simple, homely and beautiful creation of the Jewish spirit—the Kiddush! It is the very essence of poetry wrought into an institution of family life. It has cultivated and nourished the idealism of generations. It has proven a factor of incalculable worth in linking loving hearts to home, to kindred, to Israel and to God. It has given a dignity, tenderness, and grace to the Jewish household which has constrained all its influences and memories in an atmosphere of sweet religiousness. This we cannot afford to lose.

In the present era of changes many are eager to sanctify the home life by simple religious rites, and to find some way of holding fast to or restoring this beautiful custom. They would be grateful for some formula by which to give expression to the Sabbath Sentiment. To them this book is offered. It is written and compiled for their needs and in answer to a laudable "Suggestion."

It gives the formula of the Kiddush for celebrating the advent of the Sabbath eve in the home circle. The matter is the same as of old, modified to conform to the beliefs, the thoughts and tastes of to-day, but retaining the spirit that has hallowed the usage throughout many ages.

It is given in English with all directions in detail. The familiar blessings over bread and wine are retained in Hebrew with translations.

The music of one of the Sabbath Hymns is reprinted.

The book is given up largely to beautiful selections from Jewish writings containing Sabbath Legends, Poems, Songs, and an account of the Sabbath in History and in the Law.

It contains also many of the sterling Ethical Precepts which have distinguished the Sabbath as a teacher of humaneness, cheer, hospitality and domestic love.

These selections are to be used for home readings at the pleasure of the members of the household, and are presented to enkindle and to foster a deeper Sabbath Sentiment.

A Glossary explains all symbols and terms.

The poetic sentiment of this little collection of writings seemed to demand an appropriate art setting. They are therefore illustrated with engravings of the famous paintings on the Sabbath Eve by Moritz Oppenheim, also with pen and ink drawings and two full page pictures specially designed in bas-relief for this work by Miss Katherine M. Cohen, of Philadelphia.

H. B.

SABBATH WELCOME.

KIDDUSH.

HOME SERVICE FOR SABBATH EVE.

The housewife gives the family table a festive appearance. A winecup and two loaves of bread for the blessing are set before the head of the household. In the center of the table the Sabbath lights are placed. .

The ceremony of ushering in the Sabbath is begun by the kindling of these lights by the housewife, who with hands uplifted, silently asks a blessing on her home and dear ones, or uses the formula as follows:

"May our home be consecrated, Oh, God, by the light of Thy countenance. May it shine upon us all in blessing, that these lights may be to us as the light of love and truth, the light of peace and good will. Amen."

SABBATH WELCOME.

When all are seated, the master of the house says:

" Come, let us welcome the Sabbath in joy and peace !

Like a bride, radiant and joyous, comes the Sabbath. She brings blessings to our hearts. Work-day thoughts and cares are put aside. The brightness of the Sabbath light shines forth to tell that the divine spirit of love abides within our home. In that light all our blessings are enriched, all our griefs and trials softened.

13

"At this hour God's messenger of peace comes and turns the hearts of the parents to the children and the hearts of the children to the parents, strengthening the bonds of our devotion to that pure and lofty ideal of the home which is pictured in sacred writ (Prov. xxxi:10):

Whoso findeth a virtuous woman, far above pearls is her value.

The heart of her husband doth safely trust in her: he will not see his gain diminish.

She treateth him well and not ill all the days of her life.

She looketh well to the ways of her household and eateth not the bread of idleness.

She giveth provision to her household and a task to her maidens.

She girdeth her loins with strength and giveth vigor to her arms.

She spreadeth out her open palm to the poor. Yea, her hand she stretcheth forth to the needy.

She openeth her mouth with wisdom, and the law of kindness is on her tongue.

Strength and dignity are her clothing, and she smileth at the coming of the last day.

Well known in the gates is her husband when he sitteth with the elders of the land.

Her children rise up and call her blessed, her husband also, and he praiseth her, saying: Many daughters have done virtuously, but thou excellest them all.

False is grace and vain is beauty; but a woman that feareth the Lord, she alone shall be praised.

Give her of the fruit of her hands, and let her own works praise her in the gates."

"She giveth provision to her household,
And a task to her maidens."   Prov. xxxi:15

THE BLESSING OF THE WINE.

The master of the house then lifts up the wine-cup and says :

"Let us praise God with this symbol of joy and thank Him for all the blessings of the week that is gone; for life, health and strength; for home, love and friendship; for the discipline of our trials and temptations; for the happiness of our success and prosperity. Thou hast ennobled us, O God, by the blessings of work and in love and grace sanctified us by the blessings of rest through the Commandment, 'Six days shalt thou labor and do all thy work, but the seventh day is the Sabbath hallowed unto the Lord thy God.' "

בָּרוּךְ אַתָּה יְיָ אֱלֹהֵינוּ מֶלֶךְ
הָעוֹלָם בּוֹרֵא פְּרִי הַגָּפֶן:

"Praised art Thou, O Lord our God, Ruler of the world, who hast created the fruit of the vine to gladden the hearts of men."

The goblet is passed as a loving cup and each in turn drink therefrom.

THE BLESSING OF THE BREAD.

The master of the house then breaks the bread and dipping a piece in salt pronounces the blessing, saying :

—17—

בָּרוּךְ אַתָּה יְיָ אֱלֹהֵינוּ מֶלֶךְ
הָעוֹלָם הַמּוֹצִיא לֶחֶם מִן הָאָרֶץ:

"Praised art Thou, O Lord our God, Ruler of the world, who causest the earth to yield bread for the nourishment of men."

Each one at the table likewise partakes of the bread and salt.

BLESSING THE CHILDREN.

The parent with hands upon the head of each child in turn silently pronounces such a blessing as the heart may prompt, or uses the formula as follows :

"May the God of our fathers bless you!

May He who has guided us unto this day, lead you to be an honor to our family.

May He who has protected us from all evil, make you a blessing to Israel and all mankind. AMEN."

GRACE AFTER THE MEAL.

"O Lord, Thou art our Shepherd, and we shall never want. Thou openest Thy hand and satisfiest the needs of every living being. We thank Thee for the gifts of Thy bounty which we have enjoyed at this table. As Thou hast provided for us hitherto, so mayest Thou provide for us throughout our lives. Thy kindness endureth forever and we put our trust in Thee.

While we enjoy Thy gifts may we never forget the needy, nor allow those in want to be forsaken. May our table be an altar of loving kindness and our home a temple in which Thy spirit of goodness dwells. We praise Thee, O Lord, who in kindness sustainest the world. AMEN."

זכור
את־יום
השבת

The Day of Rest.

Andante con moto.

1. Come, O Sab - bath - day, and bring Peace and heal - ing on Thy wing, And to ev' - ry trou - bled breast Speak of Thy di - vine be - hest; Thou shalt rest! Thou shalt rest.

2 Earthly longings bid retire, Quench our passions hurtful fire: To the wayward, sin-oppressed Bring Thou Thy divine behest: Thou shalt rest !	3 Wipe from every cheek the tear, Banish care, and silence fear; All things working for the best Teach us the divine behest; Thou shalt rest !

(**By** permission from the "Union Hymnal," page 92.)

The family service may be brought to a close by singing the above or some other appropriate hymn.

SELECTIONS

FROM THE

LEGENDS, LORE AND SONGS
OF ISRAEL.

NOTE.—One or more of the following selections may be read aloud at the pleasure of the family gathering, sometime during the Sabbath Eve. A different selection may be made each week.

These readings will not alone afford instruction and entertainment to young and old, but give appropriate direction to the conversations and discussions of the home circle.

SABBATH LEGENDS.

"Legends express the idealism of the masses; they mirror
the spiritual life, art, poetry, science and
ethics of a people."

PRINCESS SABBATH.

In Arabia's book of stories
Read we of enchanted princes,
Who from time to time recover'd
Their once handsome pristine features.

Or the whilom hairy monster
To a king's son is converted,
Dressed in gay and glittering garments
And the flute divinely playing.

Yet the magic time expires,
And once more and of a sudden
We behold his royal highness
Changed into a shaggy monster.

Of a prince of such-like fortune
Sings my song. His name is Israel,
And a witch's art has changed him
To the figure of a dog.

As a dog, with doggish notions,
All the week his time he muddles
Through life's filthiness and sweepings,
To the scavengers' derision.

—25—

But upon each Friday evening,
Just at twilight, the enchantment
Ceases suddenly—the dog
Once more is a human being.

As a man, with human feelings,
With his head and breast raised proudly,
Dressed in festival attire,
His paternal hall he enters.

"Hail, all hail, ye halls beloved
Of my gracious regal father!
Tents of Jacob, your all-holy
Entrance-posts my mouth thus kisses!

Lecho Daudi Likras Kalle—
Loved one, come! the bride already
Waiteth for thee, to uncover
To thy face her blushing features!"

This most charming marriage ditty
Was composed by the illustrious
Far and wide known Minnesinger
Don Jehuda ben Halevy.

In the song was celebrated
The espousals of Prince Israel
With the lovely Princess Sabbath,
Whom they call the silent princess.

Pearl and flower of perfect beauty
Is the princess.   *   *   *   *

Yet the beauteous day fades quickly;
As with long and shadowy legs
Hastens on the fell enchantment's
Evil hour, the prince sighs sadly.

Feeling as though with his bosom
Icy witches' fingers grappled;
He's pervaded by the fear of
Canine metamorphosis.

To the prince then hands the princess
Her own golden box of spikenard.
Long he smells, once more desiring
To find comfort in sweet odors.

Next the parting drink the princess
Gives the prince—he hastily
Drinks, and in the goblet only
Some few drops are left untasted.

With them sprinkles he the table,
Then he takes a little waxlight,
And he dips it in the moisture
Till it crackles and goes out.

SABBATH EVE.

On Sabbath eve—thus have the sages said—
Man's homeward path, with him, two spirits tread.

The one a holy angel, pure and bright,
And one, a demon of malignant spite.

Happy the dwelling, where the day of rest
Is fitly honored as a welcome guest;

Where Sabbath-lamp doth hallowed radiance shed
Above the board, with festal dainties spread;

Where grateful hearts have sung with glad acclaim
Hymns of thanksgiving to God's holy name.

With sacred joy, the messenger of light,
With inward raging, the malignant sprite,

Behold.   The first, in tones serene and clear,
Echoes the rapture of the ancient seer:

"How lovely are the tents of Jacob's race;
Israel, how beautiful thy dwelling place!"

"Amen!' the other, with ungracious mien,
Responds; and turns to fly the unwelcome scene;

But heareth, even though he hasten flight,
In fervent blessing raised, that voice of light.

"Be every Sabbath blessed as this!" Again,
Despite his will, the demon cries, "Amen!"

But woe the household, that the holy eve
Finds unprepared its presence to receive,

The lamp unlighted, table unadorned,
With work unhallowed, God's sweet Sabbath scorned;

Where no glad heart hath chanted, "Come, O, Bride!"
—Ah, woe that thrice unhappy home betide.

Weeping, the radiant angel leaves the place
Where all unwelcome is his holy face.

The Demon of Unrest, with joy malign,
Sees him depart, and cries, "This house is mine!"

"Be Sabbath-joys forever here unknown!"
"Amen!" he hears the angel's farewell moan.

O, blessed Sabbath, of God's gifts the best,
O, Royal Bride! O, lovely Queen of Rest!

Our lamp is lighted, and its sacred flame
Shines to thy glory and thy Monarch's name.

In grateful melody, our voice we raise
To sing thy beauty and thy Maker's praise.

Would all God's people knew thy saving grace,
And thou, in all their hearts, held'st honored place.

Would all God's people, in the blessings rare,
Thy loyal ones enjoy, might weekly share!

For though stern Woe rule all the world besides,
Where Sabbath dwells, there happiness abides.

"Then come, who art thy husband's crown, in peace;
Our sorrows lighten, and our joys increase."

"Amid the faithful whom thy love hath blessed,
Come, beauteous Bride! Come, gracious Queen of Rest."

SABBATH SPICE.

A story is told of the Emperor Antoninus and Rabbi Judah the Holy. They were on friendly terms with each other, and one Sabbath the Emperor dined with the Rabbi and found the cold food very appetizing. He chanced to eat at the Rabbi's house another time—it was on a week day—and although the hot repast was varied and costly, this did not taste as well as the other.

"Wilt thou tell me, Rabbi," the Emperor asked, with a curiosity which was excusable in the monarch of Rome, "what made the cold food so appetizing?"

"There was a certain spice used in its preparation," the Rabbi replied, "which is called Sabbath, and gives every dish a pleasant flavor."

"Let me see it," the Emperor answered quickly. "I would like very much to have it used in my kitchen."

"This precious spice," said the Rabbi, "is only to be used by those who keep the Sabbath day holy."

The Ring of Polycrates—Talmudic Version

When Herodotus told about the ring of Polycrates, he hardly imagined that the Talmud could furnish a parallel. The story is a practical argument in favor of Sabbath observance. There lived once a righteous Israelite, whose scrupulous regard for the Sabbath was widely known. It was a day that he held in such high honor that he spared no cost to give it a holiday aspect. The Sabbath among the Jews was never a day of gloomy asceticism; manual labor and needless exertion were forbidden, but the atmosphere was a bright and joyous one. In the Israelite's vicinity lived a heathen of great wealth. It was foretold to the latter that his property should fall into the Jew's hands. Determined to thwart prophecy, he sold all his fortune for a precious gem, which he sewed in his turban, so that he might always have his property with him. Once, while crossing a bridge, the breeze blew his turban into the water, and with it he lost his dearly prized jewel. The next day a large fish was brought to market and as the Israelite wished to have it for his Sabbath meal, he secured it at a high price. On opening it the jewel was found, which made him wealthy for all time.

Sabbation—The Sabbath River.

Josephus in his account of the journey of the Roman Emperor, Titus, tells (Book VII–5) of the wonderful

Sabbatic River in Syria: "He saw a river as he went along of such a nature as deserves to be recorded in history. It hath somewhat very peculiar in it; for when it runs, its current is strong and has plenty of water, after which its springs fail for six days together, and leave its channels dry, as any one may see; after which days it runs on the seventh day as it did before, and as though it had undergone no change at all; it hath also been observed to keep this order perpetually and exactly; whence it is that they call it the Sabbatic River, that name being taken from the sacred seventh day among the Jews."

This natural phenomenon, which is not at all strange in physical geography, arises simply from the flowing together of the waters into a natural basin until a sufficient amount has accumulated so that the basin periodically overflows and fills the current of the dry stream.

Pliny, the contemporary of Josephus, in his Natural History (XXX, 2) refers to the same stream, but reports that it flowed six days and rested on the seventh.

The Midrash and the Talmud delight in references to this Sabbath River as though it were a holy token.

The legend of the Sabbation or Sambation occurs in divers forms and places. Eldad, the Danite, (880 C. E.) tells that when the descendants of the Levites hung their harps on the willow trees by the streams of Babylon and could not sing the songs of Zion in a strange land—the land of their exile—a cloud enveloped them and bore them off into the land of Havilah. Here they were safe, for round about them flowed a rapid stream which was impassable and served to protect them. Stones and sand were carried along in its swift current with resistless force. Thus the mighty stream rolled on in its course six days of the week. On the seventh it ceased its turbulence, but lo! a thick cloud then settled upon the waters, so that none could pass over them. Thus were the righteous and loyal-hearted kept safe from their pursuers.

THE SABBATH ANGEL.

In the folk-lore of Israel it was held that there were good spirits and bad spirits in the world, but they floated invisibly in the air, trying to make little boys good or sinful. They were always fighting with one another for little boys' souls. But on the Sabbath your bad angel had no power and your guardian Sabbath angel hovered triumphantly around, assisting your every day good angel, as you might tell by noticing how you cast two shadows instead of one when the two Sabbath candles were lighted. How beautiful were those Friday evenings, how snowy the table-cloth, how sweet every thing tasted, and how restful the atmosphere! Such delicious peace for father and mother after the labors of the week!

SABBATH LORE.

"The Law of the Lord is perfect,
   Quieting the soul;
The Precepts of the Lord are plain,
   Rejoicing the heart."

NOTE.—There is a wide-spread misapprehension among Jews as well as non-Jews, about the true character of the Jewish Sabbath. It is popularly misrepresented to be and to have been a day of rigid, severe and gloomy self-denial.

How utterly false is this notion will be found in the testimony of the Laws governing the Jewish Sabbath as an institution, and in the History of the day and its observance.

The Law of the Sabbath.

The law of the Sabbath is one of those institutions the strict observance of which was already the object of attack in early New Testament times. Nevertheless, the doctrine proclaimed in one of the Gospels—that the son of man is Lord also of the Sabbath—was also current among the Rabbis. They, too, taught that the Sabbath had been delivered into the hand of man (to break, if necessary), and not man delivered over to the Sabbath. And they even laid down the axiom that a scholar who lived in a town, where among the Jewish population there could be the least possibility of doubt as to whether the Sabbath might be broken for the benefit of a dangerously sick person, was to be despised as a man neglecting his duty; for, as Maimonides points out, the laws of the Torah are not meant as an infliction upon mankind, "but as mercy, loving kindness and peace."

The attacks upon the Jewish Sabbath have not abated with the lapse of time. The day is still described by almost every Christian writer on the subject in the most gloomy colors, and long lists are given of minute and easily transgressed observances connected with it, which, instead of a day of rest, would make it to be a day of sorrow and anxiety, almost worse than the Scotch Sunday as depicted by continental writers. But it so happens that we have the prayer of Rabbi Zadok, a younger contemporary of the Apostles, which runs thus: "Through the love with which Thou, O Lord our God, lovest Thy people Israel, and the mercy which thou hast shown to the children of Thy covenant, Thou hast given unto us this great and holy Seventh Day." And another Rabbi who probably flourished in the first half of the second century, expresses himself (with allusion to Exod. xxxi-13; Verily my Sabbaths ye shall keep * * * that ye may know that I am the Lord that doth sanctify you)—"The Holy One, blessed be He, said unto Moses, I have a good gift in my treasures, and Sabbath is its name, which I wish to present to Israel. Go and bring to them the good tidings." The form again of the blessing over the Sanctification-cup—a ceremony known long before the destruction of the Second Temple—runs: "Blessed art Thou, O Lord our God, who hast sanctified us by Thy commandments, and hast taken pleasure in us, and in love and grace hast given us Thy holy Sabbath as an inheritance." All these Rabbis evidently regarded the Sabbath as a gift from heaven, an expression of the infinite mercy and grace of God which He manifested to His beloved children.

And the gift was, as already said, a *good* gift. Thus the Rabbis paraphrase the words in Scripture, "See, for that the Lord hath given you the Sabbath." (Exod. xvi:29): God said unto Israel, behold the gem I gave you, My children; I gave you the Sabbath for your good. Sanctify or honor the Sabbath by choice meals, beautiful garments; delight your soul with pleasure and I will reward you (for this very pleasure); as it is said: "And if thou wilt call the Sabbath a delight and the holy of the Lord honorable (that is honoring the Sabbath in this way) * * * then shalt thou delight thyself in the Lord." (Isa. lviii:13-14.)

The delight of the Sabbath was keenly felt. Israel fell in love with the Sabbath, and in the hyperbolic language of the Agadah, the Sabbath is personified as the "Bride of Israel," whilst others called it "Queen Sabbath."

Thus we are told of R. Judah b. Ilai that when the eve of the Sabbath came "he made his ablutions, wrapped himself up in his white linen with fringed borders, looking like an angel of the Lord of hosts," thus he prepared for the solemn reception of Queen Sabbath. Another Rabbi used to put on his best clothes, and rise and invite the Sabbath with the words, "Come in, bride, come in." What the bride brought was peace and bliss. Nay, man is provided with a super-soul for the Sabbath, enabling him to bear both the spiritual and the material delights of the day with dignity and solemnity. The very light or expression of man's face is different on Sabbath, testifying to his inward peace and rest. And when man has recited his prayers (on the eve of the Sabbath) and thus borne testimony to God's creation of the world and to the glory of the Sabbath, there appear the two angels who accompany him, lay their hands on his head and impart to him their blessing with the words:

"And thine iniquity is taken away and thy sin purged."
(Isa. vi:7.) For nothing is allowed to disturb the peace
of the Sabbath; not even "the sorrows of sin," though
the Sabbath had such a solemn effect on people that
even the worldly man would not utter an untruth on the
Day of the Lord. Hence it was not only forbidden to
pray on Sabbath for one's own (material) needs, but
everything in the liturgy of a mournful character (as for
instance the confession of sin, supplication for pardon)
was carefully avoided. It was with difficulty, as the
Rabbis say, that they made an exception in the case of
condoling with people who had suffered loss through the
death of near relatives. There is no room for morbid
sentiment on Sabbath, for the blessing of the Lord
maketh rich, and he addeth no sorrow with it. (Prov.
x:22.) The burden of the Sabbath prayers is for peace,
rest, sanctification and joy (through salvation) and praise
of God for this ineffable bliss of the Sabbath.

Such was the Sabbath of the old Rabbis and the
same spirit continued through all ages. The Sabbath
was and is still celebrated by the people who did and do
observe it, in hundreds of hymns, which would fill
volumes, as a day of rest and joy, of pleasure and delight,
a day in which man enjoys some foretaste of the pure
bliss and happiness which are stored up for the righteous
in the world to come.

THE SABBATH IN HISTORY.

The Sabbath, conceived as a day of rest and sanctification, is undoubtedly of Jewish origin, and to the Jews the world is indebted for this grand institution.

While among the Assyrians, and a few kindred nations, the day celebrated in each week was devoted either to fasting and mourning or to sensual and dissolute pleasures, the celebration of the Sabbath among the Israelites was, or at least it became, in the course of a few centuries, a day of joyful rest from wearisome labor; a day of holiness; of elevating the mind; of cleansing the heart; of purifying the will.

This day was not devoted to Saturn, or to some other pagan deity, but it was *Shabbath La-Jehovah Elohekha*, "a Sabbath devoted to the Lord thy God;" it was *Kodesh*, sanctified, or set apart, to the service of the Lord, to the One-God of Israel and of all the world, to the Ruler of the nations, the Father of mankind.

In the first centuries following the time of Moses, the masses of the people had not risen to the heights of the pure and lofty conception of the Sabbath idea as it was taught by the divinely inspired prophets. From the words of warning and admonition and exhortation falling from the lips of several of these prophets, we must conclude that there were large numbers of people who disregarded or profaned the Sabbath.

Nearly a hundred years after the return from the

Babylonian captivity, Nehemiah bitterly complained about the profanation of the Sabbath, and from the biblical book bearing his name, we learn how he insisted upon certain measures in order to bring about a better observance of the day. But in post-biblical times, a stricter observance of the Sabbath became general, and since the fifth century, B. C. E., until the middle of the present century, the Jews, as a community, rarely, if ever desecrated the Sabbath by physical labor or otherwise. On the contrary, a spirit of extreme rigor in the manner of keeping the Sabbath grew up rapidly, and a tendency prevailed to extend to the utmost limits the practice of abstaining from labor and to follow the deductions from this law and the ramifications of the same in all possible directions.

But there was a danger lurking in this tendency; the danger that thereby the higher character of the Sabbath and its power for sanctifying the soul-life of the observant Jew might be forgotten, or at least might be pushed into the background. Happily—thus impartial history teaches us—these apprehensions proved to be groundless. The Sabbath retained its sanctifying power and influence, even among the extremest of the strictly law-abiding Jews. With a majority of the people, at least, the essence of the Sabbath was not considered to exist in the observance of the innumerable negative, talmudical and rabbinical precepts, telling us what a Jew must NOT do on the Sabbath, and the higher character of the Sabbath did not become lost among the Jews.

But, in briefly outlining the history of the Sabbath institution among Jews, should we restrict ourselves to merely looking up the old Jewish law books? No live institution can be fully understood if we study merely the written laws and ordinances concerning the same. The life of any great institution and its real character manifests itself independently of the words of books, of the letters of laws, of the sayings of old authorities. And if we now ask history, we shall soon learn that the Sabbath proved to be an institution of the greatest blessing for the Jews. It was for them, one of the means, and a very powerful one, by which the preservation of the Jews as a separate religious community was secured. The Sabbath endowed them with an unshakeable confidence in a Divine Providence, and gave them every week new strength to withstand the almost unceasing, cruel and pitiless attempts to exterminate the Jewish people and to extinguish the Jewish religion, and it kept them united as one religious denomination despite their having been dispersed over so many parts of the world and despite their having no ruling hierarchy and no other centralizing authorities. The Sabbath, together with a few other strong bonds, affected this almost miraculous perpetuation of Israel's existence.

One Sabbath day Rabbi Meir had been in the academy all day teaching the crowds that eagerly flocked to his lectures. During his absence from home, his two sons, distinguished for beauty and learning, died suddenly of a malignant disease. Beruriah, his wife, bore the dear bodies into her sleeping chamber, and spread a white cloth over them. When the Rabbi returned in the evening and asked for his boys that according to wont, he might bless them, his wife said, "They have gone to the house of God."

She brought the wine-cup, and he recited the concluding prayer of the Sabbath, drinking from the cup, and in obedience to a hallowed custom, passing it to his wife. Again he asked, "Why are my sons not here to drink from the blessed cup?" "They can not be far off," answered the patient sufferer, and suspecting naught, Rabbi Meir was happy and cheerful. When he had finished his meal, Beruriah said, "Rabbi, allow me to ask you a question." With his permission she continued: "Some time ago a treasure was entrusted to me and now the owner demands it. Shall I give it up?" "Surely my wife should not find it necessary to ask this question," said the Rabbi. "Can you hesitate about returning property to its rightful owner?" "True," she replied, "but I thought best not to return it until I had advised you thereof." And she led him into the chamber to the bed, and withdrew the cloth from the bodies. "O, my sons, my sons," lamented the father with a loud voice, "light of my eyes, lamp of my soul. I was your father, but you taught me the Law." Her eyes suffused with tears, Beruriah seized her grief-stricken husband's hand, and spoke: "Rabbi, did you not teach me to return without reluctance that which had been entrusted to our safe-keeping? See, 'The Lord gave, and the Lord hath taken away; blessed be the name of the Lord.' " " 'Blessed be the name of the Lord,' " repeated the Rabbi, accepting her consolation, "and blessed, too, be His name for your sake; for, it is written: 'Whoso findeth a virtuous woman; far above pearls is her value. * * * She openeth her mouth with wisdom, and the law of kindness is upon her tongue.' "

KING LEMUEL.

"The prophecy with which his mother instructed him."   Prov. xxxi. 1.

ETHICS OF
THE SABBATH.

"Ye shall revere every man, his father and his mother, and my Sabbaths shall ye keep."

Leviticus xix:3.

—⧪—

NOTE.—From the following selections it will be seen that the Jewish Sabbath is a practical teacher of Ethics. Its sterling moral maxims are taught through customs and observances which constitute beautiful and visible object lessons. Its power to regulate the conduct of the community and the home as well as institutions and individuals, is a moral force so vital and beneficent, that to weaken or lose the same, involves demoralizing influences whose woeful effects none can estimate.

ETHICS OF THE SABBATH.

THE SABBATH SPIRIT.—The Sabbath excels in importance and saving power all other Jewish institutions, because its central purpose is to sanctify God and to ennoble man.

Exod. xx:8.—"Remember the Sabbath day to keep it holy." The Sabbath is observed by resting from all physical labor and is sanctified by contemplating God's greatness and goodness. Exod. xx:10.—"But the seventh day is the Sabbath, in honor of the Lord thy God; on it thou shalt not do any work, neither thou nor thy son, nor thy daughter, thy man servant, nor thy maid servant, nor thy cattle, nor the stranger that is within thy gates."

DUTY OF WORK.—Work is an untold blessing to us. Without our daily tasks and interests we should soon become unhappy. But overwork is a curse. The rest of the seventh day is needed by man for his moral uplifting. The act of God resting on the seventh day, after six days of work is a pattern for man. This is by no means to be understood as though God rested in a human sense, but simply that He ceased creating and thus marked the perfection of His handiwork in beauty, usefulness and beneficence. Thus, too, once in seven

—51—

days, man should consider his work and "see that it is good."

THE DUTY OF REST.—Furthermore, man must rest on the Sabbath day, else if he goes on working without cessation he becomes a slave to his occupation. By never ceasing from his labors and never exercising the higher qualities of soul and mind, with which the Creator endowed him, he gradually sinks to the level of the brute, and loses more and more his divine likeness.

This is the deeper meaning of the reference in Scriptures to the redemption from Egyptian slavery as the basis of Sabbath observance: Deut. v:15—"And thou shalt remember that thou hast been a servant in the land of Egypt, and that the Lord thy God brought thee out from there by a mighty hand and by an outstretched arm; therefore hath the Lord thy God commanded thee to observe the Sabbath day."

THE DUTY OF CHEERFULNESS.— It is a duty to rejoice on the Sabbath ; therefore fasting, funerals and all expressions of sorrow are to be restrained.

Add to the Sabbath delights by fruits, spices, delicacies and flowers in abundance to awaken gratitude to God the Giver.

Isaiah lviii:13-14— " If thou restrain thy foot for the sake of the Sabbath, not doing thy business on My Holy Day, and if thou call the Sabbath a delight, the holy day of the Lord, and honor it by not doing thy usual pursuits, by not following thy own business, and speaking (vain) words;

"Then shalt thou find delight in the Lord ; and I will cause thee to tread upon the high-places of the earth, and I will cause thee to enjoy the inheritance of Jacob, thy father, for the mouth of the Lord hath spoken it."

As thus in the "Old Testament" we read the words of the prophet by which he reminded the people to "call the Sabbath a delight," so also in the post-Biblical literature of the Jews we find abundant evidence that for them the Sabbath was a day of cheerfulness.

Rabbi Josua, a great authority of the Talmud, said, "Let the celebration of the Sabbath be divided into two parts; one-half to be devoted to God, the other half to your own enjoyment."

Rabbi Jose said, "Whosoever keeps the Sabbath in a joyous manner, will be richly rewarded."

Rabbi Jehudah added: "Whosoever keeps the Sabbath in a joyous manner, will have all the desires of his heart fulfilled."

While the reading and study of Sacred Scriptures and of other good books was certainly highly recommended, it was prohibited to read on Sabbath certain parts of them, as e. g. the Lamentations of Jeremiah and other portions of a similar sad character. For no gloom should fill the heart of the Jew on the Sabbath, and no other sentiment should dwell therein than that of pure joy. It is well known that the precepts of Judaism laid great stress upon the sacred duty of visiting the sick and of consoling the mourner. While such acts of kindness, of sympathy and mercy were not to be neglected on the Sabbath day on account of the Sabbath, yet the Sabbath joy should be disturbed thereby as little as possible.

PERSONAL SERVICE.— Ezra ordained that preparations should be made for the Sabbath by the cleaning and refreshing of our clothes and our person.

"Prepare for the Sabbath yourself, however numerous may be your servants."

"It was a maxim of Jewish life, based on Ezekiel iv:13 that food must never be allowed to become loathsome to look upon. Many were the devices created by this maxim for adding to cleanliness and to the attractiveness of the viands. One of its most pretty results was the habit of covering the loaves with an embroidered cloth during Kiddush or sanctification over wine, which on Sabbaths and Festivals preceded the breaking of bread. This prevented the wine that might be spilled from soiling the bread."

HUMANE SERVICE.—"When life is in danger all laws are suspended, even the Sabbath if need be, must be broken."

At the siege of Jericho hostilities were not suspended even on the Sabbath (Joshua vi:15). At the time of the Maccabean revolt the rigid rule of the zealots through which many had suffered death, was set aside, and they took up arms in self-defense. (1 Maccabees ii:41.)

"All matters pertaining to charity and education may be discussed and decided on the Sabbath day, for these are not thine own affairs but God's," says the Talmud. (Sabbath 150. a.)

THE DUTY OF INTELLECTUAL SERVICE.— Rabbi Jeshua maintained that the Sabbath rest should be distinguished by reading from the sacred Scriptures and by better food than during the week.

Rabbi Jonathan ben Joseph said: "Ye shall keep the Sabbath for it is holy unto you; it is delivered into your power, not you into its power."

To the observance of this day the Jews owe the conspicuous fact that ignorance never spread among them as generally as among many other peoples.

With the Jews education and learning were at all times kept in high esteem. It became a deep-rooted usage in each city and town where Jews were living to have discourses delivered and learned debates held on the Sabbath days in schools, in synagogues, and in the meeting room of societies of various kinds.

Josephus ("Against Apion" ii:17) writes: "Our legislator, Moses, caused the people to abandon all other employments and assemble to hear the Law and to study it carefully every week;—a thing all other legislators failed to do."

Philo ("On the Sabbath") says: "On the seventh day there are spread before the people in every city, innumerable lessons in prudence, justice and all other virtues, while all listen eager for instruction, and so the lives of all are improved."

In consequence of these discourses and debates the audiences were more or less enlightened in the principles of their faith and in the doctrines and precepts of their religion. Thus to the Sabbath, too, we can partly ascribe the fact that, in that period of history called the "Middle Ages," a period which was characterized by the deep darkness of ignorance and superstition prevailing almost everywhere among the Christian nations, numerous poets, philosophers and scholars arose and flourished among the Jews.

"It is our duty to show honor to our Rabbis, teachers and leaders on the Sabbath day."—Rabbinical Maxim

HOSPITALITY.—"The Rabbi was not alone in taking to his hearth 'the Sabbath guest,' some forlorn starveling or other to sit at the table in like honor with the master. It was an object lesson in equality and fraternity for the children of many a well-to-do household, nor did it fail altogether in the homes of the poor; 'All Israel are brothers' and how better honor the Sabbath than by making the lip-babble a reality."

THE DOMESTIC VIRTUES.—The Sabbath tends primarily to sanctify the family life. As the scattered members of the family return to the house to enjoy the rest in sweet reunion with those nearest and dearest to them, they learn to appreciate more fully those who make daily loving sacrifices in their behalf. Thus does the Sabbath cement more closely each week, the bonds that bind together in loving affection all the members of the family.

When Friday evening came and they were again within the circles of their families, the Jewish people were joyful, they lighted the Sabbath lamps, they sang their Sabbath hymns, they chanted their psalms, and they forgot, once in each week, all the sorrows and cares of everyday life, all the affronts and insults which, without pity and without mercy, were heaped upon them. So at least on the Sabbath day, they felt released in body and soul from troubles and burdens.

To this is doubtless due the widely recognized beauty and tenderness of home-ties in Israel. Sabbath observance and filial piety stand in the closest relation, as indicated in the text : (Lev. xix:3).—"Ye shall revere every man, his mother and his father, and my Sabbaths shall ye keep."

SABBATH SONGS.

" In heaven there are holy chambers
Which music and song alone can open.'"
—SOHAR.

L'CHO DODI.

O, come, my beloved, to welcome the bride;
To greet the sweet Sabbath, our joy and our pride.

God's first and noblest thought wert thou,
Creation's crown and pride;
And Israel, with solemn vow,
Did win thee for his bride.

O, come, my beloved, to welcome the bride;
To greet the sweet Sabbath, our joy and our pride.

Then let us welcome her anew,
And be her coming blest,
Who never fails to bring to us
Unbounded peace and rest.

O, come, my beloved, to welcome the bride,
To greet the sweet Sabbath, our joy and our pride.

O, cast aside the daily cares,
The day of peace draws nigh,
In which the Prophet's dream fulfilled
Brings blessings from on high.

O, come, my beloved, to welcome the bride,
To greet the sweet Sabbath, our joy and our pride.

Be welcome then in peacefulness
Unto our home and hearts.
Renew within us righteousness,
Which love of God imparts.

O, come, my beloved, to welcome the bride;
To greet the sweet Sabbath, our joy and our pride.

MEDIEVAL TABLE HYMNS.

The Jewish table-songs were a bridge between the human and the divine. They were at once serious and jocular; they were at once prayers and merry glees. These table-songs belong entirely to the Middle Ages and all are later than the tenth century. On Friday evenings in the winter, the family would remain for hours round the table, singing these curious but beautiful hymns. The husband and wife would sometimes inaugurate the Sabbath with a duet sung to musical accompaniment. The quotation that follows is really a composite from several medieval table-hymns sung after the meal on Friday evenings or Saturday mornings.

> This is the sanctified Rest-day;
> Happy the man who observes it,
> Thinks of it over the wine-cup,
> Feeling no pang at his heart-strings
> For that his purse strings are empty,
> Joyous, and if he must borrow,
> God will repay the good lender——
> * * * * * *
> Let but the table be spread well,
> Angels of God answer "Amen!"
> So, when a soul is in dolour,
> Cometh the sweet restful Sabbath,

Singing and joy in its footsteps,
Rapidly floweth Sambatyon
Till that, of God's love the symbol,
Sabbath, the holy, the peaceful,
Husheth its turbulent waters.

Bless Him, O constant companions,
Rock from whose store we have eaten
Eaten have we and have left too,
Just as the Lord hath commanded,
Father and Shepherd and Feeder.
His is the bread we have eaten,
His is the wine we have drunken,
Wherefore with lips let us laud Him
Lord of the land of our fathers,
Gratefully, ceaselessly chanting,
"None like Jehovah is holy."

Light and rejoicing to Israel,
Sabbath the soother of sorrows,
Comfort of down-trodden Israel,
Healing the hearts that were broken!
Banish despair! Here is Hope come.
What! A soul crushed! Lo, a stronger
Bringeth the balsamous Sabbath.
Merciful One and all-holy,
Praised forever and ever.

SONG FOR FRIDAY NIGHT.

Thou beautiful Sabbath, thou sanctified day,
That chasest our cares and our sorrows away,
O, come with good fortune, with joy and with peace,
To the homes of thy pious, their bliss to increase!

In honor of thee are the tables decked white;
From the clear candelabra shines many a light;
All men in the finest of garments are dress'd.
As far as his purse, each hath got him the best.

For as soon as the Sabbath hat is put on the head,
New feelings are born and old feelings are dead;
Yea, suddenly vanish black care and grim sorrow,
None troubles concerning the things of to-morrow.

New heavenly powers are given to each,
Of every day matters now hush'd is all speech;
At rest are all hands that have toil'd with much pain;
Now peace and tranquility everywhere reign.

Not the choicest of wines at a banqueting board
Can ever such exquisite pleasure afford
As the Friday night meal when prepared with due zest,
To honor thee, Sabbath, thou day of sweet rest!

With thy angels attending thee, one at each side,
Come on Friday betimes in pure homes to abide,

In the homes of the faithful that shine in their bliss
Like souls from a world which is better than this!

One Angel, the *good* one, is at thy right hand,
At thy left doth the other, the *bad* Angel, stand;
Compell'd 'gainst his will to say "Amen!" and bless
With the blessing he hears the good Angel express.

That when Sabbath, dear Sabbath, thou comest again,
We may lustily welcome thee, free from all pain,
In the fear of the Lord and with joy in our heart,
And again keep thee holy till thou shall depart!

Then come with good fortune, with joy and with peace
To the homes of thy pious, their bliss to increase!
Already we've now been awaiting thee long,
All eager to greet thee with praise and with song.

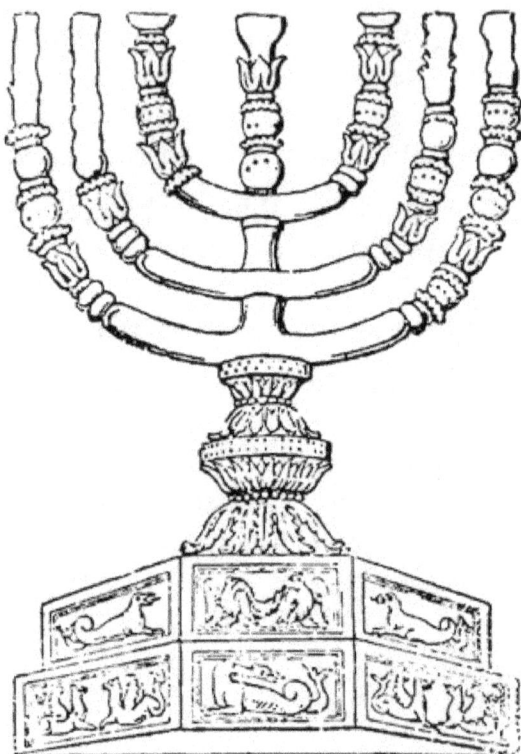

Seven-branched Candlestick, as depicted on the Arch of
Titus in Rome, among the spoils from the
Temple in Jerusalem.

THE SABBATH LAMP.

Shine, Sabbath lamp, Oh, shine with tender ray!
    Pierce the soft wavelets of the fading light;
Speed the faint footsteps of the waning day,
    And greet the shadows of the coming night.

Cast thy rays upward—cleave the darkening air,
    And lift a stream of brilliant light on high;
Shine on the wings of faith, and may they bear
    The wavering, wandering heart from earth to sky.

Fling thy rays downward—may their sacred rays
    On life's rough road of earthly travel shine;
And strew the crags that fret the rugged way
    With sparkling gems which flash a light divine!

Ah! shine afar, and may thy waves of light
    Bring near the absent dear ones far away;
Show us our loved ones in our dreams to-night,
    Our lost ones who rest in heaven's Sabbath day.

Shine, Sabbath lamp, with ray of heavenly birth,
    Emblem of faith, in hope and mercy given;
Gleam on the rude, dark path we tread on earth,
    And light our souls to find the road to heaven.

GLOSSARY.

BAAL HABAYIS.—Literally, master of the house; head of the family.

BENSHEN.—Grace after meals.

BERACHOTH (Colloquial "Berchas").—"*Blessings;*" applied specifically to the twisted loaves usually strewn with poppy seed and which are broken by the master on saying the blessing. As a mark of distinctiveness and ornamentation the loaves are wrapped in an embroidered cloth.

ESHETH 'HAYIL.—Title of acrostic in Proverbs XXXI, beginning with the tenth verse, so called from the principal words in the opening sentence meaning "a virtuous woman."

HABDALAH.—"*Separation;*" the term applied to the farewell blessings pronounced at the going out of the Sabbath, and to mark its separateness from the secular days of the week. The lighted candle, the wine-cup and the spice-box are emblems of the Sabbath joys departing.

KIDDUSH.—"*Sanctification.*" Applied to the whole religious act or service at the family table to mark the entrance of the Sabbath. Spoken of as "making Kiddush." The cup used for the blessing is called the "Kiddush cup."

L'CHO DODI.—Opening words of Hebrew hymn:

"Come, my friend," LIKRAS KALLAH, "To welcome the bride."

MENORAH.—The seven-branched candlestick, described in the Bible, used in the Temple at Jerusalem. On the Arch of Titus in Rome, among the spoils taken from the Temple, the Menorah is depicted. It is reproduced in the cut on page 68.

The Sabbath Lamp was not necessarily a "Menorah," but the favorite form is that depicted in the pictures of Sabbath Eve by Moritz Oppenheim—the hanging candelabra, having grooves for the oil, with protruding wicks.

MOTSIH.—The term by which the blessing over the bread is known, from the most important word "Hamotsih," "*Who bringeth forth* bread from the earth."

SYMBOLS.—In Jewish usage *Light* is a symbol of intellect. "The commandment is a lamp and the Law is a light." Proverbs VI-23.

Wine is a symbol of joy. "Wine maketh glad the heart of man." Psalm 104-15.

Bread serves as a symbol of all the necessaries of life. "Bread which strengtheneth the heart of man." Psalm 104-15.

These three are used as reminders of the bounty of God and visible tokens of our gratitude to Him.

CONTENTS.

NOTE.—Where the authors are not named, the articles have
been compiled from various sources.

❧ THE ❧
JEWISH CHAUTAUQUA SOCIETY.

P. O. BOX 825, PHILADELPHIA, PA.

This is a society for popular education in Jewish History and Literature. It is based on the famous Chautauqua System of Education. It has members enrolled from all parts of the Union, Canada and British India. You may enroll as an Individual Reader, a Home Circle Reader, or a Local Circle Reader, in any of the following courses:

GENERAL BIBLE COURSE.

A four years' course for the general reader and devoted to the literary and historical study of the Bible. Open to persons of all denominations and beliefs. You may begin at any time. A Syllabus, "The Open Bible," by Dr. H. Berkowitz, is provided, outlining each year's reading, and giving full directions. The completion of the four years' course secures a certificate.

Enrollment fee, 50 cents for each year.

SPECIAL COURSES
In Post-Biblical History and Literature.

Arranged by PROF. RICHARD GOTTHEIL,
of Columbia University, N. Y.

a.   From Ezra to the return of the Jews from Babylon.
b.   Origin of Christianity to completion of the Talmud.
c.   The Crusades and the Golden Era in Spain.

Other courses to be prepared covering the whole range of Jewish History.

Enrollment for each course, 50 cents.

The completion of each special course secures a seal on the Member's Certificate.

Y. F. R. U. COURSE.

"The Young Folks' Reading Union," a two years course for young people, arranged in entertaining progress by Miss Diana Hirschler. Preparatory to the General Course and leads to Y. F. R. U. Certificate.

Enrollment fee, 25 cents for each year.

The Society conducts the only Summer Assembly under Jewish auspices in the world. For Report of same, Prospectus and Circulars of Home Reading Courses,

ADDRESS HENRY BERKOWITZ,

Chancellor, Jewish Chautauqua,

P. O. Box 825,   -   -   -   Philadelphia, Pa.